Eugenio Noriega Robles

COLONIAL MEXICO

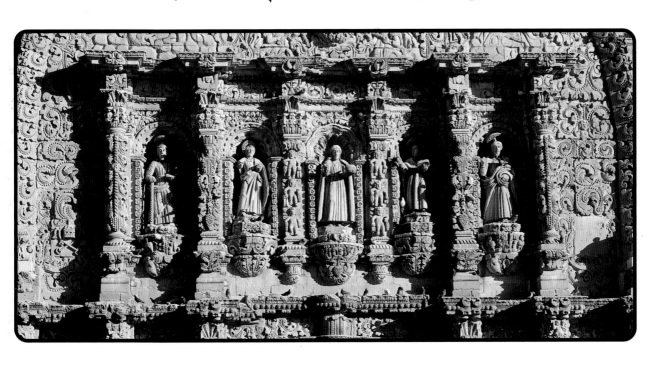

192 Color illustrations

MONCLEM
EDICIONES

BONECHI

CONTENTS

ILLUSTRATIONS OF THE COLONIAL ART IN STATES MENTIONED IN THE TEXT

TOPICS

INTRODUCTION

Columbus reached the land later to be called America in 1492 and as a result Spain began to expand its empire into this newly discovered continent. The Spanish established themselves in Cuba, from where an exploratory and trading expedition headed by Hernán Cortés set out in February 1519. Cortés landed on the east coast of Mexico on April 22 and founded Villa Rica de la Vera Cruz (today Veracruz) where he established a City Council that gave him the rank of general and authorized him to go forward in the Conquest. After a short time, Cortés left for the most powerful nation on the North American continent: that of the Aztecs. In the capital, México-Tenochtitlán, he was warmly welcomed by the tlatoani Moctezuma. Shortly afterward an uprising led by Cuitláhuac endangered the expedition; the Spanish army was defeated and had to flee and take refuge in Tlaxcala, a town that was friendly. From here Cortés, with the help of the Tlaxcalans, prepared an attack on the proud and opulent Aztec capital, which fell on August 13, 1521. Cuauhtémoc, its last sovereign, was taken prisoner and the arrogant nation lay defeated. Cortés was confirmed as Captain General and Governor of the territory that came to be known as New Spain. The capital was founded on the ruins of Mexico-Tenochtitlán, with streets laid out on a grid pattern and regular blocks of buildings. Later, Cortés was replaced as governor by Crown Officials and then by an Audiencia, or court of appeals, with a president and four judges. Expeditions were soon organized to expand Spain's dominion over what is now Mexico. After a second Audiencia a viceroyalty was established, and the court of appeals became an adjunct to the viceroy. Cities, towns and villages were governed by corregidores or alcaldes mayores (crown officials with different judicial and legislative responsibilities). An Audiencia first established in Compostela, Nayarit, in 1548 and transferred to Guadalajara, Jalisco, in 1560, was in charge of most of western Mexico, then known as Nueva Galicia. New political and administrative divisions were introduced in 1786 with the creation of Intendencias. There were 12 of these and they had the same name as their capitals. The highest officials were called intendentes, and alcaldes mayores changed their name to subdelegados. The Franciscan, Dominican and Augustinian orders took care of converting the Indians and protecting them from the abuses of certain conquistadors. Cortés himself urged the sovereigns of Spain to support and take an active interest in this effort, to send out friars for this huge and difficult task. When the first friars arrived the natives were amazed to see battle-hardened conquistadors kneel and kiss the hems of their habits. These orders worked mainly in the center and southwest. The Jesuits arrived in 1572 and conducted their missionary efforts principally in the northwest. Carmelites and the Order of Mercy arrived in 1585 and 1591 respectively. Priests who were not friars also came to New Spain. This secular clergy was under the jurisdiction of bishops, and all under that of the Real Patronato Indiano (Crown Indies Authority). The first printing house in America was established in Mexico City in 1539, and also the first university on the continent in 1553. Schools for advanced studies were established in the capital and main cities of the viceroyalty, mainly under Jesuits. The San Carlos Royal Academy of Fine Arts was established in 1783, and in 1797 the School of Mining. Viceregal society was made up of three main groups: peninsular Spaniards, Indians and Negroes, later joined by Orientals. From the intermarriage of these arose the "castes" with such strange names as lobo, tente en el aire, torna atrás or salta atrás, no te entiendo and cambujo. In other cases the names were more usual: castizo, mulato and mestizo. In 1571 the Holy Office of the Inquisition was established in Mexico City that mainly pursued transgressors of the Catholic faith. Although it is true that this tribunal was strict, its actions have been greatly exaggerated. It was finally abolished in 1820. The 18th century was a time of prosperity for New Spain. Ore mines seemed inexhaustible, and mining centers consumed huge quantities of food and industrial products from both New Spain and Spain itself. The War of Independence broke out in 1810 and spread rapidly all over Mexico, keeping the country in turmoil until 1821, when it finally separated from Spain. During the 300 years of Spanish rule, the Colonial period, a special style of art originated and flourished from the paradoxical clash and fusion of cultures but which at the same time has one particular feature: "Mexicanness."

Mexico City. The beautiful imposing facade of the cathedral (1573-1813) dominates the spacious Plaza de la Constitución.

Facing page. Mexico City cathedral. The Altar del Perdón by Jerónimo de Balbás was finished in 1732. Statues of saints and clerics and a painting that replaced one by Pereyns are contained in this altarpiece with inverted pyramid-shaped columns.

ART OF THE SIXTEENTH CENTURY

The Franciscans, who arrived in 1532-1524, the Dominicans in 1526 and the Augustinians in 1533, built churches and monasteries which, besides looking like fortresses because of their bulk and solidity, showed fine examples of art. Monasteries and their churches are the most important and representative works of the 16th-century architecture of New Spain. The Augustinian ones were magnificent, those built by the Dominicans less ostentatious, and Franciscan ones rather austere in comparison. Artistic styles — in the widest sense of the word — were successfully combined in these, some of which were in fashion at the time, such as Renaissance, with its classical elements. The interpretation of this style in Spain, very finely carved and replacing classical columns by ones made up of several sections was known as plateresque because it resembled the work of silversmiths *(plateros)* in its delicateness and rich ornamentation. To these must be added the Islamic style. Used by Arabs working for the Christian Spaniards and with influence from the latter it produced the Mudejar style. To this we owe *alfarjes* the ornately carved wooden ceilings that hid tile roofs with two or four slopes; decoration of purely geometrical designs, and the *alfiz*, a molding that almost completely surrounds the bays of doors and windows. They used bricks as a building material which they sometimes left bare, in other words without plaster and for facings they were fond of brick itself and glazed tiles. In addition to these styles the Romanesque and ogival (or as Rafael de Sanzio disparagingly called it, Gothic) also served as models. Parts were copied from the first, which

Facing page, above left. Interior of Mexico City cathedral. The central one of the wide naves terminates in the choir, like in Spanish cathedrals, with its railings of tombac and one of the organs, dating from 1736.

Facing page, above right. Mexico City cathedral. The sacristy is covered by rib vaulting with paintings — almost murals — by Cristóbal de Villalpando and Juan Correa (1684-1686).

Facing page, below. Mexico City cathedral. One of the two organs. José Navarre built one of them completely and remodeled and adapted the other (1736).

Mexico City cathedral. Sagrarium. The main facade by Lorenzo Rodríguez (1749-1768) includes inverted pyramid columns which are an important part of this baroque feature that looks like an elaborate stone altarpiece.

flourished in the High Middle Ages. From the Gothic came pointed or ogival arches and ogee arches, slender columns and although in Mexico they were mostly not functional but were purely decorative, the cross or groin vault. This is one of Gothic architecture's great inventions: to rest the vault on diagonally crossed ribs, plus other smaller ones, tiercerons, thus forming lovely complex designs, which apart from serving as a permanent intrados, directed the thrust of the vaults to four places perfectly located in the corners of the vaulted section. There are spaces of the vaults that can be seen between the ribs and the tiercerons. A large rose window makes facades look lighter and is also a symbol of the Divinity. To drain roofs the Orders installed waterspouts in the shape of monsters — gargoyles. All this was complemented by contributions from the different ethnic groups of New Spain whose artists were consummate builders, painters and sculptors. They put their techniques and tastes at the service of the conquistadors, including flat, graffito-like carving and decorations made up of regional fruit and flowers. This hybrid art of native technique applied to Spanish works has been named *tequitqui* — Ethno-European or Ethno-Christian. Reproductions of buildings in all these styles or inspired by them were used in building convent complexes, whose models came from Europe but were adapted here to local needs. Four necessary elements were added to convent complexes in Mexico, which although necessary at the time later became integral parts of Mexican churches These include especially the atriums, which are still built and used today. These elements — New Spain's contributions to world architecture — were *capillas posas,* open chapels, atrium crosss and the atriums themselves mentioned above.

ATRIUMS. These are wide spaces in front of churches and convents that were used as roofless naves for the open chapels. They were surrounded by a wall topped with merlons, with one, two or three entrances with semicircular arches, sometimes double and sometimes triple. In the atriums, which also served as cemeteries, Indians were congregated to indoctrinate them. For this boys, girls, man and women gathered in each of the corners where *capillas posas* had been built. Atriums still exist in many churches and almost all preserve their surrounding wall.

CAPILLAS POSAS. These small buildings whose name comes from the Latin verb *pausare* "to rest" or "to set down" were for processions to stop at to cense the Holy

Mexico City. National Palace (begun in 1692). The sobriety of its frontispieces in chiluca and the long front faced with tezontle (dark red volcanic stone) make this majestic building typical of 17th-century Mexico City.

Sacrament or to venerate an image carried in the procession. These strange chapels have two entrances, on the sides not built against the atrium wall, though some have only one. The finest are those of Calpan and Huehotzingo in Puebla; almost all the others are very simple. Their walls are broken with either one or two entrances with sober arches and topped with merlons, as at Yecapixtla and Totolapan in Morelos: Cholula in Puebla; Tepeji del Río and Tasquillo, Hidalgo.

ATRIUM CROSSES. Almost always, where the diagonal paths of the atrium intersected, crosses were built. They appear to have originated with a tall wooden cross that the friar Pedro de Gante ordered raised in the atrium of the great San Francisco convent of Mexico City. This

was later replaced by a stone one since its height attracted lightning. The feature pleased, and as a result stone crosses were placed in other atriums. On the shaft and arms they were carved in relief or bore graffito drawings of the instruments of the passion, in other words, those used for the crucifixion and death of the Savior. Nothing more than the face, hands and feet of Christ were shown, perhaps — as has been suggested — for fear of reminding the Indians of sacrificial victims.

Not all these crosses are in their original positions: some because the atriums have been mutilated or have disappeared, and in other cases, even when this did not happen, because they were simply moved. Standing outside the reduced atrium is the cross of Cuautitlán, State of

Mexico City. Hospital de Jesús. Founded by Hernán Cortés, it is probably the only 16th-century building in the Historic Center.

Mexico City. San Francisco church. Detail of the frontispiece. Its columns and 18th-century baroque lines show the mutilation of the reliefs of its medallions inflicted in the second half of the last century.

Mexico, the most beautiful one in existence. The one of Ciudad Hidalgo, Michoacán, which is important because at the intersection of the shaft and the arms is the cross of thorns with an obsidian disk, a survival of the pre-Hipanic custom of including this feature on the images of gods. Others show drops of blood instead of nails.

OPEN CHAPELS. These are roofed buildings with one or two arches opening onto the atrium. This in turn served as a nave, where the faithful gathered to hear services conducted in the roofed area containing the altar. There were very simple, small ones, and others that were spacious and elaborate; some were incorporated into churches themselves or the *portería* (loggia) of convents, while others were independent of both these buildings.

Mexico City. Cloister, Convent of La Merced. This is the most beautiful 17th-century baroque cloister, with its profusely decorated columns, spandrels and arches.

Facing page, above. Mexico City. Colegio de las Vizcaínas. Main courtyard. Wide corridors surround this area of the building, which has been in use for over two hundred years.

Facing page, below. Mexico City. Colegio de San Ildefonso. Courtyard of the Great College. Founded by the Jesuits in 1588, the original building was renovated from 1712 onward. This section, the work of father Cristóbal de Escobar y Llamas, was inaugurated in 1740.

Mexico City. Santo Domingo church, dedicated in 1736. Its relatively sober baroque frontispiece in chiluca stone stands out against the dark red tezontle of the walls. The columns have one third of their shafts decorated with carving and the remainder with wavy grooves.

Mexico City. Palacio de la Inquisición (1732-1736). This building by Pedro Arrieta housed the much-feared Court of the Inquisition. The courtyard has harmonious arcades and groined arches in the corners of the lower floor.

Mexico City. Capilla del Pocito (1777-1791). This a complete example, both in floor plan and construction, of 18th-century baroque, enhanced by brilliant glazed tiles. It is the work of Francisco Guerrero y Torres.

The most elaborate ones include that of Tlacolula, Oaxaca, which has a hexagonal dome supported by striated columns; the one in Coixtlahuaca, Oaxaca is similar. The one in Tlalmanalco in the State of Mexico has several arches opening onto the atrium which are covered with reliefs, almost certainly carved by native artists. They are supported by sheafs of slender columns reminiscent of the Gothic style. The one in Cuernavaca, Morelos, is in the *portería*. In Actopan, Hidalgo, it is an impressive arch at one side of the church; those of Tlahuelilpa, Hidalgo, and Acolman, State of Mexico and others look

Mexico City. Medina Picazo chapel, Regina church. This work by Miguel Custodio Durán was dedicated in 1733. At one side of the chancel is the statue of the founder, Father Buenaventura de Medina Picazo, at prayer.

13

Mexico City. Palacio de Minería. Its elegant and sumptuous architecture makes this the most important neoclassical civil building in Mexico City. The architect was Miguel Tolsá.

Mexico City. Casa de los Azulejos, residence of the Condes del Valle de Orizaba. Built around 1737, it illustrates the Mexican taste for glazed tiles.

like wide balconies or theater sets. The open chapel of Tlaxcala, Tlaxcala, standing separate from the church, with its small ogee arches, stands in a strategic position on high ground, affording ample visibility. The Capilla Real of Cholula, Puebla, deserves a special mention, since it has nine naves separated by a forest of pillars and columns that bring the Mezquita (Mosque) of Cordoba in Spain to mind. The face onto the atrium was originally open, but then was walled in, though the arches can still be made out.

Mexico City. Palacio de Iturbide. This palace, originally the home of the Conde del Jaral de Berrio, was occupied by Emperor Agustín de Iturbide for a short time, hence its name.

Mexico City. Casa de los Condes de Heras Soto. Falsely believed to have belonged to this family, the building is a classic example of a viceregal mansion.

CONVENTS. These are vast, solid buildings facing onto the atrium, to which they were communicated by the *portería* with one, two or more arches. They usually have one cloister, or sometimes two. These are corridors or galleries with barrel or groin vaults, although the latter are sometimes reserved for the corners, running around all four sides of an open patio with a garden. They could also be covered by beamed roofs. When convents have two stories, the lower one contains the kitchen, refectory, library (which could also be on the upper floor) the "de

Facing page. Tepotzotlán, State of Mexico. The church of San Francisco Javier, one of the finest examples of baroque architecture, was built between 1755 and 1757.

Tepotzotlán, State of Mexico. Capilla de Loreto. side chapel. The decoration of polychrome and gilded stucco includes an angel sculpted almost in the round.

profundis hall" so called because the gatherings held in it began with the prayer or chant from Psalm 129: *"De pro-fundis clamo ad Te, Domine...",* and other offices. On the upper floors were the cells, latrines and sometimes bathing facilities. Both these last could also be on the lower floor. Walls, cloister vaults, refectory, library, the "de profundis hall" and even cells were decorated — in some cases totally covered — with murals in black and white and in some areas in color. Behind lay the vegetable gardens, orchards, and in some cases grain stores, stables and dovecotes. The forbidding appearance of these buildings, with both atrium and church walls topped by merlons, and sometimes with guard towers, and the fact that in some cases walkways run round the outside walls of the church, which were believed to have been for patrols, led to the opinion that convents were built as fortresses against possible Indian uprisings. However, the parapets do not cover a man, the atriums are very often lower than outside, and the entrances without gates, which rules out the convents as true fortresses — defensive or offensive; they simply have the appearance.

CHURCHES. Standing at one side of the convents, these have single naves that originally had ornately carved wooden ceilings which were later replaced by vaulting. The naves usually became narrower when it reached the presbytery, to which it was connected by the "triumphal arch." The walls were covered in grisaille, and very occasionally polychrome decoration. At the entrance, above, supported by vaults, were the choirs, which in convent churches are very spacious and sometimes extended into the nave with galleries. These choirs contained the organ — when there was one — and in addition the seats used by the friars at the permitted moments during the long services. At the center stood a pyramid

Tepotzotlán, State of Mexico. Capilla de Loreto. Side chapel. Lavish decoration of gilded stucco and altarpieces set with oil paintings by Miguel Cabrera.

Facing page. Tepotzotlán, State of Mexico. Church of San Francisco Javier, finished in 1682. In the 18th century the original altarpieces were replaced by the ones now to be seen, the work of Miguel Cabrera and Higinio Chávez (1753-1754).

shaped lectern on a pedestal, which also held the large psalm books. At the end of the nave was the presbytery, so named because it was reserved for presbyters (priests). This was also where the high altar stood, and it was therefore the most important place in the church. Retables were affixed to the wall behind the altar and sometimes to the side walls and along the nave. On one of these walls is the pulpit, composed of a sort of walled balcony and a canopy to help project the priest's voice. At the sides of the high altar in some churches there are what appear to be pulpits, called ambos, from where the Epistles and the Gospel were read out. There were also churches built on a basilican plan. As well as convent churches, were built by the secular clergy and they were to be used as cathedrals — in bishoprics — parish churches and vicarages.

CONVENT CLUSTERS. The three religious orders all built them on a very similar plan. The pattern of areas, offices, buildings and architecture were much the same. Their main difference is in the degree of richness or sometimes austerity. The Augustinians appear to have favored the plateresque style of architecture, fine and elegant, like the facade of the convent church of Acolman, State of Mexico. Also plateresque, but more elaborate than the one mentioned is the facade of the convent in Yuriria, Guanajuato. The convents of Ixmiquilpan and Metztitlán, both in the state of Hidalgo, have their buildings organized like in the previous examples, but they are purist, classical. The plateresque facade of the convent of Cuitzeo, Michoacán, has more verticality than the ones above. Monumentality is the main feature of the convent of Actopan, Hidalgo, both in the proportions of

Acolman, State of Mexico. Augustinian church. The frontispiece is in the purest and most delicate plateresque style, with sectioned columns and magnificent sculptures (1560).

Facing page, above. Hacienda de San Nicolás Peralta, which originally belonged to the Carmelites. Part of the building looks like a convent.

Facing page, below left. Otumba, State of Mexico. Font. Carved from a single block by a native stonecutter in the 16th century, it is an example of tequitqui or Ethno-Christian art.

Facing page, below right. Otumba, State of Mexico. Baptismal font. Also carved from a single block of stone in the 16th century, it is the twin of the font mentioned above insofar as its decoration of twisted cords and rosettes.

Acolman, State of Mexico. The Augustinian church has a single nave, as was usual in the 16th century. Part of the vault has ribs, while mural paintings complete the decoration.

Ixmiquilpan, Hidalgo. Augustinian church. Detail of the
exceptional polychrome 16th-century mural in the nave.

Facing page, above. Actopan, Hidalgo. Augustinian church and
convent. Facade of the church with double portal, a Mudejar
tower and elegant lodge. Part of the open chapel's arch can be
seen on the left.

Facing page, below left. Actopan, Hidalgo. Augustinian church.
Fine rib vaulting covers two sections of the nave and the chancel.
Sixteenth century.

Facing page, below right. Actopan, Hidalgo. Augustinian church.
View of one side of the church with its solid buttresses topped by
large menacing lookout turrets.

Ixmiquilpan, Hidalgo. Augustinian church. The classicist
frontispiece resembles the one of Acolman in the organization
of its elements.

Actopan, Hidalgo. Augustinian convent. Detail of the decoration in the stairwell — a veritable gallery of Augustinian saints in a simulated arcade with sectioned columns.

Epazoyucan, Hidalgo. Augustinian convent. One of the 16th-century murals, Descent from the Cross, which was colored at the beginning of this century.

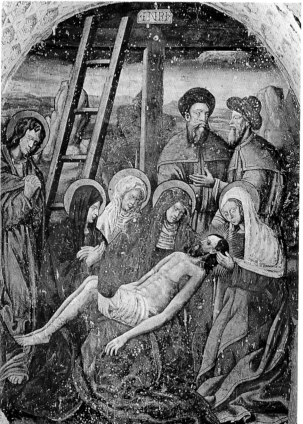

the church itself, the open chapel and the Mudejar tower. The *portería* is like a Roman triumphal arch. Richness is also apparent in the rib vaulting of cloisters, as at Yuriria, Actopan and Ixmiquilpan, with ogival arches on the lower floor and semicircular ones on the upper story. There are also those of Meztitlán and Cuitzeo, the latter with an original interplay of two arches on the upper floor to each single one on the lower. A certain degree of austerity is evident in some buildings in hot regions, as at Atlatlahuacan, Totolapan, Jantetelco, Jonacatepec and Zacualpan de Amilpas, all in the state of Morelos. In these cases, the facades are sober and the cloisters almost massive, with arches that seem pierced through the thick walls. The cloister of Yecapixtla, Morelos is of this type, but with elegant faces. On the facade there is a lovely rosette which is Gothic in style, as is the pulpit, with delicate reliefs on the panels. Most of the inside faces are

Hacienda of Teplepaya, Hidalgo. The main door is guarded by two towers with loopholes.

Zempoala, Hidalgo. Aqueduct. Also known as the Arches of Padre Tembleque, its tallest arches are approximately 40 meters high. Sixteenth century.

also Gothic in style. The Dominicans built in a more showy style, especially the convents of Yanhuitlán, Etla and Cuilapan in Oaxaca. In the first of these, the proportions of the church nave and its rib vaulting are particularly impressive, while the side face is in a vigorous plateresque style. The convent cloister, like those of the other two mentioned, is composed of lovely solid arches. In the state of Morelos, the convents of Tepoztlán and Oaxtepec are similar in the architecture of their cloisters, but differ in that of their churches. The first, in a splendid setting at the side of Mount Tepozteco, has an archaic-looking front with its figures of the Virgin Mary, St. Dominic, St. Catherine of Siena and other decoration. The facade of the convent in Oaxtepec is impressively austere. The church, with the beginnings of cross vaults, has ribs, and is generally more refined than that of Tepoztlán with its heavy barrel vault. Finally, the

Yecapixtla, Morelos. Augustinian church and convent. Facade of the church with its frontispiece and a rosette of delicate stone tracery. To the right is the loggia. Sixteenth century.

Oaxtepec, Morelos. Dominican church and convent. An austere frontispiece sparingly adorned with a simple panel around the arch. Sixteenth century.

Franciscans were restrained, building sober convents and reserving any richness for churches or other religious constructions. At Huejotzingo, Calpan, Tepeaca, Tecamachalco, Tecali, Cholula and Cuauhtinchán, all in the state of Puebla, artistic and architectural richness was applied to the churches and *posa* chapels (in the first two cases) with reliefs and carving on the facades, although some fronts are also austere, as in Tepeaca or Cuauhtinchán, the latter of classical purity. Huejotzingo has fine ribs and a magnificent altarpiece; Cholula also has rib vaulting and a facade with Gothic touches in a circular window above the entrance, and Romanesque ones in the cornice. The convent cloisters of all of them are sober, and almost all have beamed ceilings. The church of Tlaxcala expresses Franciscan poverty with its facade and severe doorway in the shape of a semicircular arch enclosed by a panel, and above, the window of the choir. The nave, however, has an extraordinary richly

carved wooden ceiling, which is the only one of its size still existing in Mexico. On the shores of Lake Pátzcuaro in Michoacán the Franciscan convent churches of Tzintzuntzán and Erongarícuaro have large shells on their facades. In the former, one serves as the splayed arch of the apparent niche over a window divided by a slender column. Lastly, in Yucatán, the churches of Maní and Izamal have smooth facades topped by belfries or belfries and towers. The atriums are vast, the one of Izamal surrounded by long rows of graceful arches on plain, slender pillars. These convent groups were the bases for unending and exhausting missionary and cultural work carried out by the friars. This is why they are set in places that were strategic at the time for evangelization and in towns that were heavily populated before, but now contain few inhabitants (except Morelia, Michoacán, and Puebla, Puebla, where there are 16th-century convents).

Cuernavaca, Morelos. Palacio de Cortés. Although altered, it is an example of palatial 16th-century mansions. The tower on the left was added later.

Tepoztlán, Morelos. Dominican church. This part of the frontispiece contains the flattened reliefs of angels, the Virgin Mary, Dominican coats of arms, initials and other elements. Sixteenth century.

BASILICAS. These originated in Roman buildings for trade, composed of three naves, the central one higher than the others, separated by rows of arches. The front had three entrances, and at the rear there was an apse. After issuing the Edict of Milan in 313, the emperor Constantine ceded these buildings to the Christians for holding their services. They were altered for this purpose so successfully that they were adopted as models for churches. The apse was reserved for priests, while the naves were for the faithful. Not only were existing structures used, but others were built. We shall mention three 16th-century basilicas in Mexico belonging to convents. Only small parts of the convent complex in Tecali,

*Taxco, Guerrero. Parish church of Santa Prisca.
The choir, with its balustrade and beautiful 18th-century
baroque organ.*

*Taxco, Guerrero. Parish church of Santa Prisca.
The facade of the church which the wealthy mine owner José
de la Borda had built by the architect Cayetano de Sigüenza.
Spiral columns were still used on the frontispiece. Eighteenth
century.*

Puebla, remain but the basilica is the finest of the three.
The central doorway is in along graceful Renaissance
lines. Inside, the three naves are separated by slender
columns carrying semicircular arches, and the whole interior is very open, since the high altar can be seen clear-
ly from any angle. It originally had an ornate carved
wooden ceiling, but this was destroyed in the last century. In Santiago Cuilapan, two towers and belfries on
round bases stand at the ends of the main facade, and the
interior is not open like in Tecali because as it is in an
area prone to earthquakes, the columns and arches are
sturdy. Semicircular openings in the side walls lighten
them and provide ventilation in this hot region. The
basilica of San Pedro and San Pablo (St. Peter and St.
Paul) in Zacatlán de las Manzanas, Puebla, has a facade
topped by crenellation. The front is completely classic in
style. Double columns flank the entrance of a semicircular arch, entablature and a triangular pediment. The inte-

Taxco, Guerrero. Parish church of Santa Prisca. Detail of one of the highly ornate Churrigueresque altarpieces.

Tlaxcala, Tlaxcala. Sanctuary of Ocotlán. The baroque facade with its work in mortar. Eighteenth century.

Tlaxcala, Tlaxcala. Sanctuary of Ocotlán. Dome of the Lady chapel with baroque plaster decoration. Eighteenth century.

Facing page, above. Tlaxcala, Tlaxcala. Franciscan church and convent. In the foreground, part of the open chapel; in the background, the free-standing bell tower. Sixteenth century.

Facing page, below left. Tlaxcala, Tlaxcala. Franciscan church and convent. The impressively simple monolithic baptismal font. Sixteenth century.

Facing page, below right. Tlaxcala, Tlaxcala. Franciscan church. The lovely ceiling of carved wood over the nave. Sixteenth to seventeenth century.

rior is divided into three aisles separated by rows of arches and between them the ceiling has a series of circular medallions reminiscent of the Basilica of St. Peter in Rome.

OTHER SIXTEENTH-CENTURY ARCHITECTURAL WORKS

WATER MANAGEMENT. The oldest aqueduct in Mexico is the Tembleque of Zempoala, Hidalgo, so named for Father Francisco de Tembleque who built it between 1554 and 1571 to carry water from some springs near Zempoala to Otumba in the State of Mexico. It has some 126 arches, some of which are very high (40 meters). Natural springs were a vital source of water at the time. Also dating from the 16th century is the aqueduct of Tochimilco, Puebla, in which the columns are supply points. The central one is topped by a shield. A veritable water tank because of its size is the one of Teapulco, Hidalgo. There were also fountains in convent

Above left. Puebla, Puebla. Cathedral. The facade with its "Herrerian" towers and three doorways. Seventeenth century.

Above right. Puebla, Puebla. Cathedral. Main or detached altar. This neoclassical work was planned and begun by Manuel Tolsá in 1797 and finished by the architect José del Manzo in 1819.

Facing page. Puebla, Puebla. Cathedral. Altar de los Reyes. This work in alabaster (Mexican onyx) is by Pedro García Ferrer, who also painted the pictures. This altarpiece was perhaps the first one to include spiral columns (1645-1646-1649).

Puebla, Puebla. Cathedral. Dome and side aisles with coffers that decrease in size as they rise. giving the impression of greater height.

Puebla, Puebla. Cathedral. The sacristy. The two canvases that embellish this area — The Triumph of Faith and The Triumph of Religion — are by Baltasar Echave Ibía.

Puebla, Puebla. Cathedral. Choir stalls inlaid with precious wood, ivory and bone in Mudejar designs (1719-1722).

cloisters, such as in Huejotzingo and Tochimilco, Puebla, and Ocuituco, Morelos. The latter is one of the lovliest, but the most important because of its size and monumentality is the public fountain in Chiapa de Corzo, Chiapas, built of bricks, with the structure showing, after Mudejar taste.

DWELLING HOUSES. Few remain from this century. The best preserved are the Palacio de Cortés in Cuernavaca, with its loggias; the Mazariegos house in San Cristóbal de las Casas, Chiapas, with a small plateresque facade; the Palacio Montejo in Mérida, with its splendid plàteresque portal, and finally a splendid building in Meztitlán called "La Tercena" with outlooks onto fertile meadows. Only the facade and small portions of the Casa del Dean de la Plaza remain in the city of Puebla. The portal is entirely Renaissance in style. There must also be a few properties in the cities of Puebla and Cholula that are not preserved entirely. Other works

worth mentioning are the "Rollo" in Tepeaca, a tower on an octagonal base that rises on the wide Plaza Mayor or Plaza de Armas of Tepeaca, similar to the Torre del Oro in Seville. Mudejar influence can be seen, and it possibly served as a watchtower as well as being a spire.

PAINTINGS. Pre-Hispanic peoples knew the techniques of fresco and tempera, but not oil and easel painting, which were introduced by the Spanish. The conquistadors also contributed the ideas of perspective and volume which were completely unknown in pre-Hispanic painting. No doubt some of the native painters (*Tlacuilo* in Nahuatl) who studied art in the San Francisco school established by Fray Pedro de Gante in Mexico City were responsible for decorating the convents established in certain regions of New Spain. So, the beginnings of colonial art lie in the mural decorations of convents, which most probably existed in all, although some have been destroyed or covered by several coats of whitewash.

Puebla, Puebla. Santo Domingo church. Dome of the Rosary chapel. In the center is the dove of the Holy Ghost, surrounded by symbols of the Seven Gifts and Divine Grace (1690).

Puebla, Puebla. Santo Domingo church. Rosary chapel, inaugurated in April 1690. Its exuberant plaster decoration is yet another expression of the baroque.

Facing page, above. Puebla, Puebla. Church of the Company of Jesus. Dedicated in 1767, it is the work of the architect José Miguel de Santa María. The towers are later additions (1804-1812).

Facing page, below. Puebla, Puebla. Former Jesuit college. The baroque hall. Like the Rosary chapel, its vault is covered with plasterwork. Stalls complete the decoration. Seventeenth to eighteenth centuries.

Puebla, Puebla. Palafox Library. In 1646, Bishop Juan de Palafox y Mendoza donated his library to the College of San Pedro. In 1771, Bishop Fabián y Fuero added to the book collection and built the present location, which was inaugurated in 1773.

They were usually painted in black and white, though there are some examples in different colors. The barrel vault in the refectory of the convent of Actopan has coffers decorated with colors. The walls of the nave of the convent church in Ixmiquilpan, Hidalgo, has striking polychrome decoration of native warriors wearing crown-like headdresses and carrying weapons that include wooden paddles edged with razor-sharp obsidian blades, who are presumably fighting against evil. All this mural art in convents, particularly in the *porterías* was not only decoration, but also had a didactic purpose. The first European painter we have information about — the Fleming, Simon Pereyns — arrived in 1566. Andrés de la Concha, a native of Seville came to Mexico in 1568, and by 1580 the Basque, Baltasar de Echave Orio was in the lands of New Spain. These are the three most important figures in the painting of New Spain in the second half of the 16th century.

They all employed oils and the technique of tempera on board. In their works, figures wear angular robes: De la Concha's style is softer and more delicate than Pereyns's; his Madonnas express gentleness. This can be appreciated by comparing *La Sagrada Familia* (The Holy Family) and *Santa Cecilia* (St. Cecilia) in the Viceregal Art Gallery *(Pinacoteca Virreinal)* or his works on the altarpiece of Yanhuitlán with the Flemish artist's paintings on the retable of Huejotzingo. De la Concha's coloring is more delicate, and the positioning of hands more sensitive. Echave Orio was the founder of a school of painting, and sometimes his figures are more rigid and the clothing stiffer, as in the *Resurrección de Cristo* (Resurrection of Christ) in the Guadalajara Museum.

Puebla, Puebla. Casa de los Muñecos or de los Gigantes. An example of Puebla architecture in brick and glazed tiles. Eighteenth century.

Puebla, Puebla. Casa de Alfeñique. The rich stucco decoration resembles twisted sugar candy ("alfeñique"), hence its name. Eighteenth century.

Huejotzingo, Puebla. Franciscan church and convent. The usual sobriety of Franciscan buildings did not mean that this frontispiece could not be adorned with slender columns and medallions containing the initials of Christ and the Virgin Mary. Sixteenth century.

Above, right. Huejotzingo, Puebla. Franciscan church and convent. Detail of one of the posa chapels, with an angel of the Passion and twisted cord decoration. Sixteenth century.

Calpan, Puebla. Franciscan convent. A posa chapel. The Virgin Mary with seven broadswords, the flat carving — almost engraved designs — the decoration, the pyramid-shaped vault and the pinnacle — a cactus — reveal the hand of a native artist in this first chapel. Sixteenth century.

Facing page, above. Cholula, Puebla. Capilla Real. Domes and elevated groined vaults topped by small lanterns (1661-1731) form the roof of this exceptional chapel.

Facing page, below. Cholula, Puebla. In 1594, a hermitage was built on the top of a pre-Hispanic pyramid and later became a chapel. The building was destroyed in an earthquake, and the church to be seen now dates from the last century.

Cholula, Puebla, Capilla Real. A forest of columns and pillars, like in the Mosque of Cordoba, Spain, supports the vaults.

Although his Revelations are more profound, the clouds forming them look solid. Trained in the European school — though apparently in subjects and forms, not techniques — the *tlacuilo* Juan Gersón left paintings dealing with biblical themes on *amate* (bark paper) which were affixed to the vault in the lower choir of the church of Tecamachalco, Puebla. Another famous *tlacuilo* not to be forgotten was Marcos de Aquino Cipac.

SCULPTURE. Sixteenth-century statues generally show serene figures; their clothing hangs almost vertically and the elegant folds are angular, while the adornments are often magnificent. Fortunately, other figures survive in addition to those on altarpieces. These include a Virgin Mary with the Christ child on her lap in the National Viceregal Museum of Tepotzotlán in the State of Mexico. This is an archaic style throned Virgin who neither connects with nor looks at the Child, while Christ is a typically Renaissance *bambino*. In the same museum there is a stone statue also of the Madonna and Child. She wears voluminous, heavy clothing while He is almost naked. There is a gentle fluidity to the figures. There are two more excellent figures, one in the Santa Mónica Museum of the city of Puebla and the other in temple-museum of Cuauhtinchán, Puebla. Both are of St. Anne, the Virgin Mary and the Christ Child in a single group. The adornments are rich, and the carving delicate. Some statues dating from this century are highly venerated nowadays, such as the Virgin of Ocotlán, Tlaxcala, Nuestra Señora de Santa Fe in the city of Guanajuato, and others.

41

State of Puebla. Church of Santa María Tonantzintla. This is a native version of the Rosary chapel in the city of Puebla. The decoration shown is in plaster. Eighteenth century.

State of Puebla. Church of Santa María Tonantzintla. Detail of the interior decoration. Cupid-telamons, masks and other elements make up the multicolored decoration.

Facing page. State of Puebla. Church of Santa María Tonantzintla. The nave, cross vaults and dome are covered with flowers, fruit and plants between cupids and masks. It can all be compared to tlalocan (a pre-Hispanic paradise) but is Christian. Eighteenth and nineteenth centuries.

CORN STALK FIGURES. This pre-Hispanic technique is one of New Spain's contributions to world art. The body of the statues was formed of dried corn stalks stuck together with glue and with either rods or circles of wood inside the hollow body. Others were fashioned from paper soaked in a glue solution similarly with a hollow inside. The outside was covered with dry cornstalk pith then with paper soaked in thin glue. Made by one of these techniques, the figures were covered in plaster mixed with glue and then painted. In the National Viceregal Museum there is a lovely Christ on the Cross, made of cornstalk, which is completely Renaissance in style. The expression is calm, and blood is not over-used. The famous Señor de Santa Teresa, which was the object of so much veneration, is also made of cornstalks, as are Nuestra Señora de la Salud of Pátzcuaro, Michoacán, the Señor del Cacao in Mexico City cathedral, and others. The National Viceregal Museum recently acquired an ex-

ceptional cornstalk figure — possibly of St. Mary Magdalene or the Virgin Mary — made using the first technique mentioned above.

RETABLES (ALTARPIECES). The word retable derives from the Latin *retro*, behind, and *tabula*, panel. Altarpieces originated in the tablets that even in the 5th century A.D. were placed before altars. These were then positioned behind and above, and later became triptyches, then polyptyches, and finally elaborate altarpieces. Construction of these required the services of either one or two artists to plan the project and sculpt and paint the images necessary, as well as a number of craftsmen to prepare, carve and assemble the wood and then cover it with gold leaf. Altarpieces evolved in accordance with the prevailing styles of art. There are two magnificently proportioned Renaissance ones. The first is in the Franciscan church of Huejotzingo, where puristic ele-

Above left. State of Puebla. Church of San Francisco Acatepec. A beautiful almost unique facade covered with polychrome and brilliant glazed tiles. Eighteenth century.

Above right. State of Puebla. Church of San Francisco Acatepec. Like Tonantzintla, the inside of this church is filled with stucco work (recently restored).

Cuauhtinchán, Puebla. Franciscan church, interior. This plateresque altarpiece is in the chancel. Sixteenth century.

Tecamachalco, Puebla. Franciscan church. A tlacuilo (Indian artist) who assumed the name Juan Gersón painted these biblical scenes on bark paper which were affixed to the vault of the lower choir. Sixteenth century.

Tecamachalco, Puebla. Franciscan church, interior. Monolithic font carved by a native stonecutter. An example of tequitqui or Ethno-Christian art. Sixteenth century.

ments are combined with plateresque sectioned columns and decorations of cupids, garlands or festoons. The altarpiece and statues are the work of Pedro de Requena, and the paintings are by Simon Pereyns. In addition to its beauty and artistic value, it is full of religious symbolism. The altarpiece of Xochimilco in Mexico City is purer, without sectioned columns and has paintings attributed to Baltasar de Echave Orio. There are other altarpieces, not of these dimensions but equally important, such as those in the churches of Cuauhtinchán and Tecali, Puebla, and in Texcoco, State of Mexico.

FEATHER MOSAIC. This technique, dating from pre-Hispanic times, was also one of New Spain's contributions. It consisted of creating figures and designs with

Port of Veracruz, Veracruz. Fort of San Juan de Ulúa. The need to protect the port from any kind of attack led to the construction of these fortifications.

small brightly colored feathers on a background that could be cloth, thin copper plaques or bark paper *(amate)*. The feathers were stuck on with the sap of a certain species of orchid, and the surface of mosaics look like velvet. This technique was used to produce such images as Christ Giving His Blessing in the National Viceregal Museum, the finest surviving example known, and a St. Andrew in the parish church of Calpan. The same method was used for liturgical articles such as miters, chasubles, dalmatics, and even sacring tablets (inscriptions with the words of consecration particularly) which were placed on altar tables. One of these was recently recovered from abroad and is now in the National Art Museum of Mexico City.

CATHEDRALS. A cathedral — a name derived from the Latin *catedra,* chair — is the main church of a diocese (from the Greek *dioikesis*, government) which is the territory governed by a bishop (from the Greek *episcopos,* guardian). The first diocese to be created in Mexico was the *Carolense* in 1519, with its seat on the island of Cozumel, which was at first thought to be part of the mainland. Years afterward it was moved to Tlaxcala and finally to Puebla (1539). Other dioceses were established and cathedrals built in their capitals. The only one dating from the 16th century is that of Mérida, Yucatán, which was completed in 1598. Its ground plan is rectangular and its three naves are roofed by groined vaults all of the same height. The facade is high, wide and very sober.

Querétaro, Querétaro. Aqueduct. The Marqués de la Villa del Villar del Aguila had this built (1726-1735) to supply water to the Capuchin convent and the city as a whole.

Querétaro, Querétaro. Casa de Ecala. One of the finest facades of houses belonging to the colonial bourgeoisie, with its lovely wrought iron balconies. Eighteenth century.

Mexico City cathedral (1573-1813), the most beautiful, richest and most monumental in Latin America, has a central nave, two lateral naves, and two with chapels. The central nave ends with the choir. Baroque and neo-classical altarpieces grace the chapels. Puebla cathedral (1575-1649-1768) which also has five naves with a choir in the central one. The interior has a neoclassical unity that was given to it in the last century. The cathedral of Oaxaca (1610-1730-1736), similarly with five naves, still has the choir in the central nave, like the cathedrals mentioned earlier. The building is sturdy and low since it is in a region prone to earthquakes. In San Cristóbal de las

Facing page, above. Querétaro, Querétaro. Santa Rosa church and convent. This is a typical nunnery church with its single nave running parallel to the street onto which its two doorways open.

Facing page, below. Querétaro, Querétaro. Santa Rosa church. Sacristy. A large oil painting with an arched top adorns the sacristy. Statues of the apostles top the chests of drawers. Eighteenth and nineteenth centuries.

Querétaro, Querétaro. Santa Rosa church. The upper and lower choirs, with their railings and the richly gilded fan with an oil painting of the twelve apostles, splendid altarpieces and a pulpit with exquisite inlaid work are all in the nave.

49

Above left. Querétaro, Querétaro. Interior of Santa Rosa church.

Above right. Querétaro, Querétaro. San Francisco convent. The austere but attractive 17th-century cloister.

Querétaro, Querétaro. San Francisco church. The choir, with one of the finest surviving lecterns known (1792-1795).

Querétaro, Querétaro. Convent of San Francisco. Staircase connecting the two stories.

Above right. Querétaro, Querétaro. Casa del Marqués. The baroque lines of this 18th-century mansion illustrate the taste that colonial aristocracy had for this style.

Querétaro, Querétaro. Neptune Fountain. Although the neoclassical arch is the work of Tresguerras, the statue of the god is not. It probably dates from years earlier.

Querétaro, Querétaro. Convent of San Agustín. A detail of the lovely 18th-century cloister. The building is now a museum.

Casas, the cathedral has the ground plan of basilica, with modifications inside. The facade is baroque, with work in mortar (1718-1721). The vaults of Guadalajara cathedral (1561-1618) are of the same height, and it has beautiful classic doorways. The choir was destroyed in the last century, and other alterations were made. Morelia cathedral (1640-1744) has austere doorways, very tall towers, and three naves without chapels. The lower choir was destroyed in the 19th century. Durango cathedral (1635-?) is a fine building with three naves and doorways with spiral columns, The cathedrals of Mexico City, Puebla and Durango still have their beautifully ornamented choir stalls.

SEVENTEENTH AND EIGHTEENTH-CENTURY ART

In the late 16th century, innovative tastes appeared in art. In 1563, Philip II of Spain ordered the architects Juan de Toledo and Juan Herrera to build the palace-monastery-tomb of El Escorial. This monumental complex, majestic and austere, of a "sad solemnity" marked the beginning of the short period of very plain style of architecture in which pure, well-ordered lines predominate and which was called *herreriana* ("Herrerian") or *escurialense* (Escorial style). In Mexico City, its influence can be seen in the rear faces (1615) of the cathedral, as well as those that give onto the lateral naves, both of the chapels, the sacristy (1623) and the chapterhouse. The latter ones with impeccable lines without any decoration. Puebla cathedral also shows this influence in its towers, even though one was finished in 1678 and the other is later, but they are the most *Herrerian* towers to be found in Mexico.

THE BAROQUE

The word baroque, which designates a period in art, comes from the Portuguese *barroco* the name given to an irregularly shaped pearl. The word was not applied to architecture as an adjective until the late 18th century to mean extravagant or over-extravagant. This was the

Querétaro, Querétaro. Santa Clara. The austere lines of the Herrera style persist in the frontispiece of this nunnery church. Seventeenth century.

Above right. Querétaro, Querétaro. Santa Clara. The inside of this church looks like a golden grotto, despite the austere facade. Eighteenth century.

Querétaro, Querétaro. Creativity ran riot in this frontispiece-tribune of carved and gilded wood and wrought iron. Eighteenth century.

Querétaro, Querétaro. Missions of the Sierra Gorda. Concá, the work of Brother José Antonio Murguía, who was here from 1748-1767.

Facing page. Concá. The beautiful facade bears a large Franciscan coat of arms and is crowned by a very rare sculpture of the Holy Trinity. 1754-1762.

opinion of lovers of neoclassicism, and for some time it was considered as excessively ornate art in bad taste. Only recently has baroque art been appreciated. The pioneers were the Italian architects Lorenzo Bernini and Francesco Borromini. The first of these two built the baldachin of the papal altar in the Basilica of St. Peter in Rome (1625-1633), giving rise to the baroque style. In this work he used columns with spiral shafts, inspired by one from the temple of Solomon in Jerusalem, which is why they are known as Solononic. This new style of art and architecture spread to New Spain, where it was welcomed enthusiastically. It should be remembered that in the 17th century the Viceroyalty was in full economic swing, thanks to the political and social stability that had almost been achieved and to the enormous production of silver. This wealth led to the proliferation of buildings in the new style, to alterations of existing ones. At the beginning, colonial baroque was discreet and sober; it began by breaking pediments and adding some decoration to purist buildings, then gradually changed the classical rules by interrupting friezes or making them bend or break. During the course of the 17th and 18th centuries, there were different expressions, modes and variations. It was also during these periods that three architectural innovations appeared in New Spain: domes, churches on a Latin cross plan, and nunnery churches.

State of Querétaro. Missions of the Sierra Gorda. Landa. The frontispiece, where the central lane is wider than the side ones. The first level has pilasters standing in niches (1760-1768).

Facing page, below left. State of Querétaro. Missions of the Sierra Gorda. Jalpan. Work of Brother Junípero Serra, now Beatified. Fine ornamentation completely covers the frontispiece, which displays special interpretations of estípite columns (1751-1758).

Facing page, above. State of Querétaro. Missions of the Sierra Gorda. Tilaco, the work of Brother Juan Grespi. This detail of the facade shows the choir window with a gallery of draperies and some cherubs supporting the crown. 1754-1762.

Facing page, below right. State of Querétaro. Missions of the Sierra Gorda. Jalpan. Detail of the frontispiece with a statue of San Francisco in a niche.

Guanajuato, Guanajuato. Alhóndiga de Granadillas. This was built between 1798 and 1809 to serve as a grain warehouse, and was the setting for one of the most important battles in the War of Independence.

Above right. Guanajuato, Guanajuato. The church of the Company of Jesus. The facade has three frontispieces with finely carved baroque columns. Eighteenth century.

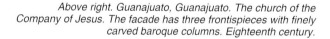

Left. Guanajuato, Guanajuato. General view. The basilica- parish church stands in the foreground and behind it is the modern University building.

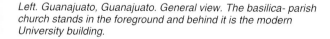

Guanajuato, Guanajuato. Church of the mining town of Cata. The enormous output of silver financed the construction of this fine baroque church. Eighteenth century.

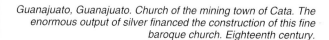

Above left. Guanajuato, Guanajuato. La Valenciana church. The lavish main frontispiece presages the richness to be found inside: altarpieces with baroque estípite columns, an exquisitely inlaid pulpit and paintings by Luis Monroy. Eighteenth and nineteenth centuries.

Above right. Yuriria, Guanajuato. Augustinian church. This frontispiece was built along the lines of Acolman's, with sectioned columns, but the decoration distinguishes it. Sixteenth century.

Dolores Hidalgo, Guanajuato. A magnificent frontispiece with Churrigueresque columns, and two towers make up the facade of this church. It was here, in the atrium, that Father Hidalgo sparked off the independence movement on September 16, 1810.

Yuriria, Guanajuato. Detail of the frontispiece of the Augustinian church with small angels playing musical instruments and, on the choir window, sectioned columns. Sixteenth century.

NUNNERY CHURCHES. These have a special layout. Although these institutions were founded in New Spain in the 16th century, the first one being La Concepción in Mexico City (1530-1540), the church itself was built in the 17th century. They are constructed along the street, and access is usually through two doorways in the wall of the nave that leads outside.

At the foot of the naves there were two choirs, which the nuns used for holding or attending divine services. These choirs give onto the nave through openings protected by grilles. The lower one is double and has small "windows" at the sides through which the nuns received Holy Communion without leaving the choir. Underneath the lower choir there is a crypt with an ossuary and tombs for nuns. The presbytery is the same as in other churches; there stood the high altar, and very occasionally the lower choir opened in its side walls. Fortunately, several nunnery churches survive, though not the one of La Concepción, which like many others was destroyed as a result of the Reform Laws. Those in Mexico City include San Jerónimo (1623), Regina (1573), Balbanera (1663), Santa Teresa la Antigua, Santa Teresa la Nueva. In Puebla, there are Santa Rosa, Santa Mónica and Santa Clara. In Guadalajara, Capuchinas and Santa Mónica survive, and in Lagos de Moreno, also Jalisco, Capuchinas. In Querétaro, Santa Clara, Santa Rosa de Viterbo and Teresitas. In Morelia there are the churches of Santa Rosa, Las Monjas and Capuchinas. San Juan del Río, Querétaro, is perhaps the only place where the original nunnery and church both still stand, and the church of La Concepción in San Miguel de Allende, Guanajuato, part of whose former convent was inhabited by nuns.

EVOLUTION OF THE BAROQUE. We have seen that the baroque style was moderate and discreet at first, but gradually more and more ornamentation was added and it grew in volume and at the same time changed the rules of classical orders. So, the two or three stages of some doorways are almost flat, but in others, the first stage is plain and the upper stages have columns instead of pillars. In many cases, one third of the shaft of these columns is decorated. Then, Solomonic columns made their appearance, with many variations in the form of the

San Miguel de Allende, Guanajuato. Church of San Felipe Neri.
In addition to the interesting facade and the paintings
and statues inside, the outstanding feature is the
Loreto chapel and its side chapel.

Left. Panoramic view of San Miguel de Allende, Guanajuato.
This was one of the richest towns in the Viceroyalty, and its
houses and churches, especially those dating from the 18th
century, illustrate what towns were like during this century.
The facade is 19th-century neo-Gothic.

spiral, ranging from the simple ones with shafts that twist on themselves, to the Bernini style, in which the helixes are covered with decoration, particularly plants, the columns which mark their deeply sunken spirals with vines, ones that mark spirals with vines on a plain shaft, and those that leave these helixes with vines hollow. Spiral columns were at first used in the upper stages, and finally on all the portal. Examples of all the above are the main doorways of the Franciscan churches of Xochimilco in the Federal District and San Jerónimo in Mexico City (1613), where the arches of the doorways penetrate the entablatures. There are doorways which have pillars almost without volume, including those of La Encarnación church (1639-1640) in Mexico City; those of San Francisco and Santa Clara in Querétaro, and of the parish church of the city of Guanajuato (1696). Reliefs were also often placed on the second stage of doorways, and the first were perhaps those of La Encarnación church in Mexico City.

In the Santuario de Guadalupe or Congregación (1675-1680) in Querétaro there are not only columns but also very early inverted pyramid shaped pillars. It appears that spiral (Solomonic) columns were first used in New Spain in 1645 on the altarpiece of the Kings. Shortly afterward, classical columns with Tuscan capitals and stri-

Salamanca, Guanajuato. Augustinian church. A large canvas with an arched top and the crucifix are part of this church with baroque altarpieces.

Celaya, Guanajuato. Church of El Carmen. This is the work of Francisco Eduardo Tresguerras, a native of Celaya, who achieved an admirable balance of neoclassic style in this church. Nineteenth century.

ated shafts on the first stages, and on the second, a central column with a third part decorated with zigzag grooves and lateral spiral ones. These are believed to be the first ones of this type in the city. The panels of reliefs in the three are essentially symbolical. Following the lovely example of the cathedral, the Barefoot Carmelite nuns had the twin doorways of their church of Santa Teresa la Antigua built (1678-1684) with spiral columns

Aguascalientes, Aguascalientes. Cathedral. Built between 1704 and 1738, it has a facade with spiral columns. The pediment with a baroque cornice dates from 1883, and one of the towers from the present century.

on the two levels and stone decoration on spandrels and entablature: instead of panels there are window openings on the second levels, which are topped by a triangular broken pediment which leaves space for the base of a statue. In San Francisco, Guadalajara (1684-1692) the facade, composed of a large semicircular arch, contains the portal with spiral columns on the two levels and in the niche. The church of La Soledad in the city of Oaxaca (1689) has a facade in the baroque taste that moves on different planes as if they were the panels of a folding screen. This intelligent solution creates more space for niches, statues and columns of different types, including spiral ones. San Agustín in Mexico City (rebuilt from 1692 onward) has a fine large rectangular relief framed by spiral columns. San Francisco in the city of San Luis Potosí (c. 1700) has twisted columns on the two levels, like the cathedral (1670-1718). Fluidity was given to the front planes of the doorway — though not as freely as in La Soledad of Oaxaca — which, like the towers have different types of spiral columns although one dates from 1910. We have seen how the taste for spiral columns spread and how they became a generalized element on facades in their different forms. These helicoidal supports are at their most splendid on the facade of Zacatecas cathedral. Vines wind up the columns, covering them with leaves, flowers and bunches of fat grapes. Spiral columns are also a striking feature of the portal of Aguascalientes cathedral (1704-1738). Finally, we may

Above left. San Luis Potosí, San Luis Potosí. Church of El Carmen. Facade. One of the richest examples of Mexican baroque (1747-1764), the first level of the frontispiece has one type of spiral columns.

Above right. San Luis Potosí, San Luis Potosí. Church of El Carmen. This magnificent frontispiece, known as the Frontispiece of the Archangels, is the "most sumptuous and excessively florid Mexican baroque work" (1787-1792).

Right. San Luis Potosí, San Luis Potosí. Cathedral. Building apparently lasted from 1674 to 1718. The frontispiece has several levels with spiral columns, which are also present on the towers (one dates from 1910).

San Luis Potosí, San Luis Potosí. The Water Tank in a neoclassical style was attributed to Tresguerras for many years.

Zacatecas, Zacatecas. The Apostolic College of Guadalupe began as a hospice in 1702. It was officially founded by Brother Antonio Margil de Jesús in 1707.

Left. Zacatecas, Zacatecas. Panoramic view of the city. This urban complex of beautifully carved pink quarrystone, intricate balcony railings in wrought or strip iron, streets, alleys, squares and gardens is dominated by church towers and domes.

mention the churches of Santa Mónica (founded in 1720) of Guadalajara, Jalisco, and San Agustín (1731-1745) in Querétaro. The doorways of the first have spiral columns, some decorated with grape vines and bunches of grapes, and others with extremely fine carvings. In the second case, the doorway is composed of twisting stone columns, octagonal in cross-section. This was another style of Solomonic column a taste which lasted until the end of the 18th century and even beyond, as can be seen in the churches of Santa Prisca, Taxco, Guerrero, Santiago Tianguistengo (1755-1797), State of Mexico, and San Felipe Neri in the city of Querétaro (1786-1805). In the first two, the spirals are along traditional lines, while in the third they are variations.

Facing page, above. Zacatecas, Zacatecas. San Agustín convent. The convent and church were rebuilt in the mid 18th century, the church being dedicated in 1782. The cloister is original in its beauty.

Facing page, below. Zacatecas, Zacatecas. The Aqueduct of El Cubo supplied water to the city for over a hundred years.

Zacatecas, Zacatecas. Cathedral. This began as a parish church in 1718 and was dedicated in 1756. The dome was rebuilt in 1848, while one of the towers dates from 1782 and the other from 1912. It was raised to the status of cathedral in 1862.

OTHER EXPRESSIONS OF THE BAROQUE. In the late 17th century, a new form of Mexican baroque art made its full-blown appearance in the Rosary chapel (1690) of the Santo Domingo church of Puebla: the use of stucco (plaster on the interiors and mortar on the exteriors). This covers the inside, filling the walls, vaults and dome with elaborate polychrome and gold decoration, which looks wonderful. A native version of this plasterwork is the inside of the church of Santa María Tonantzintla in the state of Puebla, where a riot of multicolored fruit and flowers covers the walls, vault and dome like a pre-Hispanic paradise or *Tlalocan*. This type of work in stucco is also to be found in Tlaxcala, the State of Mexico, Puebla and Chiapas. In the first of these states, the facade and interior (especially the robing room) of the Sanctuary of Ocotlán (1671-1791) just outside the state capital are decorated with this delicate, complicated work. In the city of Oaxaca, the spacious nave of Santo Domingo church (1572-1666 is covered with trailing vines, medallions, bows and sashes, medium and high reliefs. The cathedral and Santo Domingo church in San Cristóbal de las Casas, Chiapas have mortar decoration on the outside. It can also be seen in the Texcoco area, State of Mexico, on the outsides of the churches of Papalotla, Chiconcuac and Santa María Tulantongo. The glazed tiles used to cover walls and facades, yet another decorative element, help to emphasize the baroque features of buildings with their brilliance and

Zacatecas, Zacatecas. Cathedral. Detail of the facade. The top part of this imposing pediment covered in stone decoration shows God Almighty on his throne of Divine Majesty holding the globe in one hand and giving his blessing with the other.

Zacatecas, Zacatecas. Cathedral facade. A petrified forest where vines of local quarrystone wind up the columns in sinuous lines. The Savior and the Apostles appear amongst them.

color. The facades of the churches of San Francisco Acatepec, Puebla, and of neighboring Tlaxcalanzingo are good examples of this. As regards civil architecture, the same feature can be seen on the Casa de los Azulejos, *(House of Tiles)* in Mexico City and forming figures on the Casa de los Muñecos or Gigantes *(House of the Dolls or the Giants)*, as well as on other facades in Puebla.

Guadalajara, Jalisco. The cathedral. Begun in 1561, it was dedicated in 1618. The three classicist frontispieces were carved in 1599, while the pinnacles of the towers were added between 1851 and 1854.

Guadalajara, Jalisco. Church of San Felipe Neri by Pedro José Ciprés, begun in 1752 and finished in 1802. The frontispiece and towers are totally baroque.

ESTIPITE BAROQUE. The second decade of the 18th century had still not ended when in the capital of the Viceroyalty, a new type of support made its appearance that was more ornamental than structural. This was the *estípite* — a pillar composed of a base, an inverted pyramid or prism, moldings, a cube, more moldings and a capital. This pillar, which has been rightly called "the

Guadalajara, Jalisco. The Hospicio Cabañas, which Bishop Juan Ruiz de Cabañas had built. The design and plans are by Manuel Tolsá. The pediment and the dome and drum foreshadow neoclassicism.

Facing page. Guadalajara, Jalisco. The Hospicio Cabañas. What used to be the Hospice chapel was decorated by the Mexican muralist José Clemente Orozco in 1939.

great sign in form of the baroque," had precedents in Greece and Rome. It was rescued from medieval oblivion during the Renaissance, but it was Benito de Churriguera who first used it in Spain in 1689, in a funeral pyre, and this was no doubt what inspired Jerónimo de Balbás with the idea for an altarpiece in Seville cathedral. He made it fashionable in New Spain with the altarpiece for the Capilla de los Reyes in Mexico City cathedral. This masterpiece of Mexican baroque art and world gem is in the shape of an enormous niche inside the apse chapel. Four monumental *estípites* — the tallest in the world — support, or appear to support, this structure of carved and gilded wood. Two smaller ones seem to form another large niche. Another work by Balbás is the altarpiece of the Capilla del Perdón (1732). More and more altarpieces were created, and soon this type of pillar moved onto the outside of religious buildings to grace

portals. The first experiments seem to have been on the Archbishop's Palace and the College of San Ildefonso, both in Mexico City where, still plain and discreet, they are engaged. However, when Lorenzo Rodríguez built the Sagrario Metropolitano between 1749 and 1768, the *estípite* emerged triumphant on the two levels of the facade. This was the real beginning of success. Altarpieces and facades replaced earlier ones, or completely new ones were constructed in churches and other buildings. La Santísima Trinidad, San Francisco and other churches in the city were filled with excellent altarpieces that included *estípites*, and these pillars were repeated in stone on exteriors in vigorous facades and even towers, which were later imitated in the rest of the Viceroyalty. In Tepotzotlán, State of Mexico, the wealthy Jesuits built the exceptionally fine facade and tower, as well as the altarpiece, of the San Francisco Javier church belonging to

Zapopan, Jalisco. Sanctuary and College of Our Lady of Zapopan, an old village near Guadalajara. The sanctuary was finished in 1730, but the towers date from the 19th century.

Facing page, above. Morelia, Michoacán. With the object of creating jobs for the poor, in 1785 bishop Antonio de San Miguel initiated a series of public works which included this aqueduct (1785-1789).

Facing page, below. Morelia, Michoacán. Patio of the Palacio Clavijero. This is an example of the Jesuit custom of using arches on the lower level and windows on the upper one.

San Juan de Los Lagos, Jalisco. A very important trading center because of the fairs held in the Viceroyal period, it is now a major attraction for pilgrims due to the statue of the Virgin Mary that is worshiped here.

Morelia, Michoacán. The cathedral. Building was begun in 1660 and finished in 1744. Despite this, it does not posses either the spiral or inverted pyramid columns characteristic of the baroque of the times.

Facing page. Morelia, Michoacán. The cathedral. Covered by a baldachin, the silver monstrance, unique in Mexico, proudly displays its metal and workmanship. Eighteenth century.

Morelia, Michoacán. Main frontispiece of the cathedral. The austere lines mean that the architectural features are almost level with the face of the wall, without volume or movement.

Morelia, Michoacán. The cathedral. The choir with its monumental organ.

Morelia, Michoacán. The cathedral. This silver baptismal font is also unique in Mexico and illustrates the wealth that Morelia cathedral originally had.

the novitiate. In the rich mining town of Guanajuato, the Jesuits erected their church with three naves, and the three corresponding doorways have finely decorated *estípite* columns. Similarly, the Count of La Valenciana had a church and altarpieces created in this fashionable style, and even in austere Valladolid (now Morelia), members of the Order of Our Lady of Mercy built the facade of their church with simple, but disengaged, *estípite* columns. The facade of the former Palacio de la Audiencia (now the Government Palace) in Guadalajara, Jalisco has a facade with a striking doorway, and two no less striking *estípite* columns flank the central balcony. The clock tower, which also has them, dates from 1885. Also, we should mention the exceptional sacristy of San Francisco church and the Chapel of Aránzazu dating from the mid 18th century, the latter now part of the Regional Museum., where there are sturdy *estípites*. Finally, there is the country house of the Counts of the Valley of Orizaba, known as "The House of the Masks," in Mexico City. Built between 1766 and 1771, it has fine *estípites* with a young warrior figure. The taste for these

pillars spread, and even modest properties sported them proudly, such as in Jeréz, Zacatecas, where the Town Hall has disengaged *estípites* flanking the entrance.

OTHER TYPES OF ARCHITECTURE. Premises were also built to house schools, hospitals and hospices. The pattern in almost all of them was spacious cloisters (in Jesuit establishments, rows of arches were usual on the lower floor, and window openings on the upper one) onto which rooms or halls opened, the inevitable chapel, and auditoriums in boys' schools. Those in Mexico City included the Jesuit schools of San Pedro y San Pablo, El Real, and the oldest of all, San Ildefonso (1712-1740). For girls there were Las Vizcaínas (1734-1752), the Colegio de Niñas and La Enseñanza, of which only the church remains. Buildings of former Jesuit schools still stand in the cities of Querétaro, Puebla, Morelia, San Luis Potosí and Zacatecas. Sixteenth-century hospitals include the much modified Hospital de Jesús, founded by Hernán Cortés, the one of San Juan de Dios (rebuilt several times, and now the Franz Mayer Museum), both in

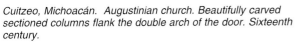

Cuitzeo, Michoacán. Augustinian church. Beautifully carved sectioned columns flank the double arch of the door. Sixteenth century.

Above right. Cuitzeo, Michoacán. Augustinian church and convent. The Renaissance style arches of the loggia have engaged columns. Sixteenth century.

Cuitzeo, Michoacán. Augustinian convent. Detail of one of the 16th-century paintings.

Facing page, above. Erongarícuaro, Michoacán. Franciscan convent church. Choir window with dividers and decorative shells. Sixteenth century.

Facing page, below. Tzintzuntzán, Michoacán. Augustinian church and convent. The plateresque frontispiece stands out against this plain facade without towers. Sixteenth century.

Oaxaca, Oaxaca. Santo Domingo church and convent. The facade of the church with its squat towers displays a frontispiece that is already in the baroque taste. Seventeenth century.

Mexico City, and others in different cities, such as the almost intact one of Atlixco, Puebla. Other works for social welfare were carried out, such as aqueducts and public fountains. Aqueducts remaining are the ones of Querétaro (1735), Zacatecas (late 18th century), Morelia (1785-1789), and the monumental one of *El Sitio* near Tepotzotlán, State of Mexico (1764-1854). Public fountains include the Salto del Agua in Mexico City, with a pair of fine engaged spiral columns. The original is now in the National Viceregal Museum of Tepotzotlán. Some magnificent examples of 18th-century mansions originally belonging to noble families survive. These are large, sumptuous buildings — especially the facades showing the family coat of arms — which always had a private chapel. In Mexico City there are the houses of the

Counts of Santiago Calimaya (City Museum), the Marquis of Jaral de Berrio, and the Count of the Valley of Orizaba. In Querétaro are the houses of the Marquess and Escala; in Durango, the one of the Count del Valle del Xuchil; in Guanajuato, of the Marquis of San Juan de Rayas and of the Count of Casa Rul; in San Miguel de Allende, the palatial residence of the De La Canal family, and in Tepic, Nayarit, the baroque house of Counts of Miravalle (Regional Museum).

BAROQUE ALTARPIECES. As we have seen, altarpieces were created in accordance with the prevailing fashion and showed development in both spiral and inverted pyramid *(estípite)* columns, of which there are several versions. Some of the earliest are in the Chapel

83

Oaxaca, Oaxaca. Santo Domingo church. Baroque plasterwork covers the inside of the church. Seventeenth century.

Facing page. Oaxaca, Oaxaca. The altarpiece in an imitation of Salomonic baroque was created between 1956 and 1959 to bring the whole together. The original was destroyed in the last century.

Oaxaca, Oaxaca. Santo Domingo church. The choir. Part of the plasterwork with a figure in high relief. Seventeenth century.

Oaxaca, Oaxaca. Santo Domingo church. The vault of the lower choir is decorated with the family tree of Santo Domingo de Guzmán.

Below left. Oaxaca, Oaxaca. The Rosary chapel in Santo Domingo church. Spiral columns flank the image of the Virgin of the Rosary. This modern altarpiece was blessed in 1964. The statue dates from the 18th century.

Oaxaca, Oaxaca. Santo Domingo church. Rosary chapel. The dome is decorated with plasterwork, and in the center is the Virgin presenting the rosary.

86

Oaxaca, Oaxaca. Santo Domingo church. Detail of walls and vaults with baroque decoration, some of the most beautiful in Mexico. Seventeenth century.

of San Cosme y Damián in Mexico City cathedral. These are to be found on the front altarpiece, which can be dated about 1650-1660. Its ornamentation is both rich and discreet; the fine carving and the outlining of its gilded motifs in black place it at the beginning of the Mexican baroque. In the same cathedral is the main altarpiece of the chapel of Nuestra Señora de la Soledad, whose spiral columns are still discreet, a feature which denotes its early date. The richest and most striking group of altarpieces with spiral columns is in the chapel of San Miguel, or of the Santos Angeles, which was rebuilt in 1713. The altarpieces with spiral columns frame canvases by Juan Correa dating from 1714. The main altarpiece (1688-1690) in the church of Santo Domingo, Puebla, despite being monumental, is soberly decorated. The main altarpiece of the Augustinian church in Meztitlán, Hidalgo, which was begun in 1696, has spiral columns covered in grapevines on its various levels. A

similar feature can be seen on the portal of La Soledad church in Oaxaca. Other excellent examples of Solomonic altarpieces are the one in the Franciscan church of Tlalmanalco, State of Mexico, which used to be in the nave but is now in the presbytery; that of the Dominican church of Amecameca, State of Mexico, and of San José, both with baked statues but no paintings. In the church of Yanhuitlán, Oaxaca (also Dominican), the main altarpiece, which is notable for the movement of its planes, must date from either the late 17th or early 18th century, and is one of the most striking examples of the Solomonic style and of Mexican baroque art in general. The fashion for *estipite* baroque, also known as Churrigueresque, was a tremendous success in New Spain. All who could change the Solomonic facades and altarpieces of their churches, or those who built new ones, did so in conformity with this style, which also had variations. These ranged from simple *estípites* with

Oaxaca, Oaxaca. The cathedral frontispiece is flanked by sturdy bell towers built to resist earthquakes.

Oaxaca, Oaxaca. La Soledad church. The frontispiece, which covers almost the whole facade, has different planes, a baroque device that enlarges the surface available for decoration.

cleanly contoured elements to those that covered them all with decoration and softened their lines; from those timidly engaged in walls, to bold, free-standing ones; others replaced the cubic shape with a bulbous body. Later they became niched pillars and finally merged into the structure of altarpieces in what in known as *anástilo*, in other words a style devoid of columns or pillars. The first altarpieces with inverted pyramid columns were the ones — no longer existing — in San Sebastián church, Mexico City, which were constructed between 1727 and 1728. The ones in the sacristy of San Francisco church, Toluca, State of Mexico, were created in the same period, and have similarly disappeared. These were followed in 1732 by the altarpiece in the Capilla del Perdón of Mexico City cathedral, while at the same time the one in

Yanhuitlán, Oaxaca. Dominican convent. Arcade of the lower cloister with rib vaulting. Sixteenth century.

Yanhuitlán, Oaxaca. Dominican church and convent. Front of the 16th-century church with a 17th-century frontispiece.

Facing page, above. Cuilapan, Oaxaca. The basilica. The arches divide the rectangular floor plan into three aisles. Sixteenth century.

Teposcolula, Oaxaca. The open chapel has Renaissance elements. Sixteenth century.

Facing page, below. Cuilapan, Oaxaca. The basilica. Low towers flank the frontispiece, while the side walls have arched openings for ventilation. Sixteenth century.

the Capilla de los Reyes, also in the cathedral, was being completed. It was perhaps its grandiose lines that put the seal on the taste for this new type of pillar. So, the walls of churches and chapels became covered in retables with types of *estípites* such as the beautiful complexes in those of San Francisco Javier, Tepotzotlán, State of Mexico; Santa Prisca, Taxco, Guerrero; the Augustinian church in Salamanca, Guanajuato; La Valenciana, near the city of Guanajuato, which partly illustrate the variety in *estípites*, as do those in the nunnery churches of Santa Clara and Santa Rosa in the city of Querétaro. They are not only made of profusely carved and richly gilded wood but also of stone, as in the church of El Carmen, San Luis Potosí, "the most sumptuous and excessive

work of Mexican baroque," and in alabaster (onyx), such as the spiral columns in the church of San José Chiapa, Puebla, and in the cathedral of the same city.

PAINTING. The painting of New Spain had various limitations that confined it to religious subjects, portraits, representations of the "castes" (mixed races), still-lifes and city scenes. These and court motifs were painted on folding screens, which also included scenes of the Conquest. Very occasionally, a mythological event was portrayed, such as *Flora con sus asistentes antes de una bacanal* (Flora and her Assistants before a Bacchanal) and *Muerte de Procris* (Death of Procris) by Antonio Enríquez, signed and dated 1735. Large paintings of the

San Cristóbal de las Casas, Chiapas. Santo Domingo church. Spiral columns and mortar decoration make up this facade.

Below left. San Cristóbal de las Casas, Chiapas. Santo Domingo church. One of the baroque altarpieces, part of the complex that covers the walls of the nave.

San Cristóbal de las Casas, Chiapas. The house of Luis de Mazariegos (erroneously called the house of Tobillas). A simple but dignified plateresque portal with a window flanked by sectioned columns. Sixteenth century.

San Cristóbal de las Casas, Chiapas. The facade of the cathedral has three frontispieces with two levels. On the first there is a curious arrangement of semicircular arches, and very thin mortar decoration on the three doors. 1718-1721.

Above right. San Cristóbal de las Casas, Chiapas. The beautifully carved pulpit and its supporting telamon.

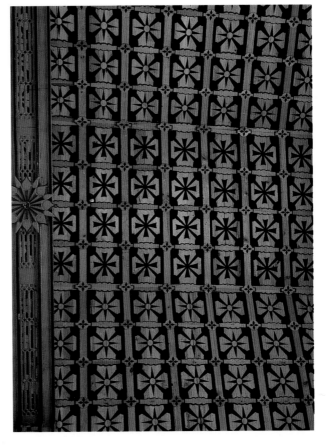

San Cristóbal de las Casas, Chiapas. Detail of the coffered ceiling with Mudejar style decoration.

Chiapa de Corzo, Chiapas. One of the most important examples of Hispano-Arabic art is this fountain built of carved bricks. It was begun by Fray Rodrigo de Laón in 1557 and finished in 1562.

Facing page, above left. Mérida, Yucatán. The only cathedral to be finished in the 16th century, it has three Renaissance style doorways.

Facing page, above right. Mérida, Yucatán. House of Francisco Montejo, the conqueror of Yucatán, with its plateresque portal. Sixteenth century.

Facing page, below. Mérida, Yucatán. The church of San Juan Bautista dates from the 17th century and was rebuilt in the 18th.

lives of the Savior, the Virgin Mary or Saints filled the cloisters or stairwells of convents or colleges, and sacristies (including Mexico City, Puebla and Guadalajara cathedrals). Excellent artists flourished in this restricted circle during the 17th century, for example Baltasar Echave Ibía, known for his use of different shades of blue for backgrounds. Other artists painted people vigorously and expressively and handled chiaroscuro — the influence of Zurbarán and José Rivera — masterfully. Examples are Sebastián López de Arteaga and Pedro Ramírez. Alonso López de Herrera is exquisite in his details, and Diego de Borgraf paints the backgrounds or surroundings of his figures with pleasure and delicacy. There was Luis Juárez and his angels with wavy, almost unkempt, golden hair, and the expressive Juan and Nicolás Rodríguez Juárez. Juan Correa, a prolific artist, dresses his angels luxuriously, and Cristóbal Villalpando

sometimes with inspired brushstrokes, and at others with magnificently careless ones. These last artists can be classed as the last representatives of the golden age of colonial painting. In the 18th century, composition became looser, although this was offset by excellent, careful draftmanship and fresh, delicate coloring. Four artists all very similar in their composition, coloring and weakness in their portrayal of personages lived and worked through a large part of this century: José de Ibarra (1688-1756), Miguel Cabrera (1695-1768), Francisco Antonio Vallejo and José de Alcíbar. The best known of these is Miguel Cabrera. There was hardly a city in Viceregal times that did not possess one of his works, and there is no good painting that is not attributed to him. The beauty and gentleness of his Virgins characterize him, while he left some excellent portraits. Andrés López, Francisco Martínez (also a gilder), and José de Páez should not be

Izamal, Yucatán. Franciscan convent and church. Long rows of arches surround the enormous atrium of this complex. Sixteenth century.

Facing page, above. Maní, Yucatán. Franciscan church and convent. The architecture is austere, like most buildings of this religious order. Sixteenth century.

Facing page, below. Dzidzantún, Yucatán. Franciscam church. This restored church, here seen from the apse, has a massive, solid look. Sixteenth century.

forgotten. There were also distinguished artists in provincial cities: in Puebla, José Joaquín Magón, Juan Tinoco and Miguel Jerónimo de Zendejas and in Guadalajara Antonio Enríquez (active between 1735 and 1749) and Diego de Cuentas.

STATUES. The baroque statues of New Spain were in fierce competition with those brought from Guatemala, which almost always overtook local production. There were also ivory figures imported from the Orient. However, noteworthy figures were carved here with rich adornments: the clothes fall gracefully, and hands and facial features are delicate. Among the most notable sculptors were José Antonio Villegas Cora and José Zacarías Cora in Puebla, and in Querétaro Ignacio Mariano de Casas and Francisco Martínez Gudiño.

NEOCLASSICAL ART. The spread of new ideas in the second half of the 18th century, Academies and boredom with the baroque, which seemed to have no future, led art to seek different forms. The explorations of Pompeii and Herculaneum that began in 1748 gradually revealed the world of two cities buried under the ash and lava of Vesuvius. They attracted taste to classical forms, to a new classicism: neoclassicism. It began cautiously in New Spain, with the introduction of elements into baroque works, but suddenly blossomed, with the result that new works were created and the baroque — now considered vulgar — was swept aside. The Valencian sculptor Manuel Tolsá arrived in Mexico bringing support to modern trends which the Mexican, Francisco Tres Guerras, was already very enthusiastic about. He and Tolsá produced the most important neoclassical works in Mew Spain. Tresguerras designed the Palacio de Minería (1797-1813), which is in fact a veritable palace in its architecture and monumentality, the mansions of the Marquis del Apartado and the Count of Buena Vista, the high altars of Santo Domingo and La Profesa churches (destroying the baroque ones), and works in the cathedral. All these are in Mexico City. The high altar in

Durango, Durango. The elaborate choir stalls of the cathedral. Seventeenth century.

Chihuahua, Chihuahua. The cathedral. This was built as a parish church between 1725 and 1760. The portal with detached columns is in a vigorous baroque style. It was raised to the status of cathedral in 1891.

Durango, Durango. The cathedral. Side portal with spiral and two estípite columns. Eighteenth century.

José Juárez. Apparition of the Virgin and Child to St. Francis. A profusion of figures with gentle expressions fills the canvas, leaving no room for landscape or architectural setting. At the bottom is a small boy, most probably the donor's son.

Below left. Don Antonio de Mendoza. An excellent portrait of the first viceroy of New Spain by an unknown artist. National History Museum, Chapultepec Castle.

Antonio López de Herrera. Divine Countenance. Each hair on the Savior's head and in his beard seems to have been painted individually with meticulous care. Seventeenth century.

Sor Juana Inés de la Cruz wearing habit and shield or medallion, ready to go to the choir. National History Museum, Chapultepec Castle.

Below. Baltasar de Echave Ibía. Portrait of a Lady. Modesty, virtue and great dignity are shown in this portrait of an aristocratic lady of the viceregal period (possibly the wife of a viceroy). Seventeenth century. Pinacoteca de Virreinal de San Diego, Mexico City.

Puebla cathedral (1797-1819) was created by other artists. Ignacio Castera and Agustín Paz were responsible for Loreto church (1809-1806-1816) with its impressive dome, while Miguel Constansó built the Crown Tobacco Monopoly now known as the Ciudadela (1807) and the cloister of La Encarnación convent on the site where the Ministry of Education now stands. He also drew the plans for the City Hall of San Luis Potosí. Tresguerras also built the Teresitas church in Querétaro (1803-1806), El Carmen in Celaya (1802-1807), La Enseñanza School in Irapuato (1810), while the house of the Count of Casa Rul has recently been attributed to Tolsá. Tolsá also designed the plans for the Hospicio Cabañas in Guadalajara. Almost all churches gradually replaced their baroque retables by cold, neoclassical altars, which are mostly lacking in value of any kind. In sculpture, the best exponent of this new trend was Tolsá, who first carved and then cast in bronze one of the finest equestrian statues in the world: that of Charles IV, popularly known in Mexico as "El Caballito" (The Little Horse). He also carved several images of the Virgin Mary and busts of important personalities of the time.

Baltasar de Echave Orio. T.
Prayer in the Garden. An ar
comforts the exhausted Sa
Sixteenth century. Pinacote
Virreinal de San Diego,
Mexico City.

Unknown artist. Christ bound to the Column. A figure full of pathos that makes exaggerated use of sores and blood. Eighteenth century. Parish church of Nuestro Señor del Desmayo, Salvatierra, Guanajuato.

Ivory Christ. These figures, brought from the Orient by the Manila Galleon (Nao de China), were not uncommon in the viceregal period. Eighteenth century. Private collection.

Our Lady of Sorrows. An image wearing richly embroidered robes. Eighteenth century. Church of St. Augustine, Salamanca, Guanajuato.

Don Pedro Ruiz de Ahumada. One of the finest and rarest of funerary figures is this one of a benefactor of the Jesuit novitiate college in Tepotzotlán. Seventeenth century. National Viceroyal Museum, Tepotzotlán. State of Mexico.

St. Lucia. Polychrome figure carved in wood. Eighteenth century, Franz Mayer Museum, Mexico City.

MUSIC AND LITERATURE. Not much colonial music has been investigated, but composers are known. We shall mention some who distinguished themselves particularly in religious music, and also cite examples of their secular works. The dates refer to the periods when they were active. Hernando Franco (1575-1585) left compositions for voice such as *Sancta María yn ilhuicac cihuapille* (St. Mary, Queen of Heaven), one of the oldest motets known (1599) and a *Magnificat*. José de Loaysa y Agurto set verses by Sor Juana Inés de la Cruz to music. The opus of Antonio de Salazar (1688-1715) includes numerous masses, Te Deums, motets, etc. Manuel de Sumaya 1708-1739) wrote the melodrama *El Rodrigo* in 1708 and saw the premiere of his opera *La Parténope* — the first one to be written in Mexico — in the viceroyal palace of Mexico City. There are two works by Ignacio Jerusalem (1739-1769): *Alegres Luces del Día* and *Cuando la Primavera*. At the beginning of the 19th century Manuel Arenzana composed Mexico's second opera

(as far as is known) *El Extranjero*, whose first performance was given in the theater that still stands in the city of Puebla. The works of great and not so great European composers were known and performed, including those of Giacomo Facco, who is forgotten in Europe. The fashionable dances of the Old World were included in court music, and this seems to be where the sarabande and chaconne originated.

In New Spain, Bernardo de Balbuena wrote the most beautiful poem ever dedicated to Mexico City, *Grandeza Mexicana* (1602-1604). The Augustinian friar Miguel de Guevara (1585?-1646?) wrote the sonnet *A Jesús Crucificado*, which has been attributed to several other authors, and the sonnet *El Tiempo y La Cuenta*, where an elaborate play on the words "cuenta" (count) and "tiempo" (time) produces one of his finest poems. The gem of Mexican literature is Sor Juana Inés de la Cruz (1651-1695), the author of numerous exquisite poems, verses and theatrical works of universal significance. There is

Equestrian statue of Charles IV of Spain. This work by Manuel Tolsá is considered one of the finest of its kind. Plaza Manuel Tolsá, Mexico City.

also the erudite scholar Carlos de Sigüenza y Góngora (1645-1700). Another figure who should be mentioned is the Guatemalan born but Mexican educated 18th-century Jesuit Rafael Landívar and his lovely poem *Rusticatio Mexicano* (Through the fields of Mexico) in which he describes the viceroyalty of New Spain.

WORK IN GOLD, SILVER AND OTHER METALS. It would be strange if a country producing gold and more especially silver, and with an ancient tradition of metalworking, had not used these minerals for both coins and works of art. There were many of these, but they were melted down later for their intrinsic value, to be convert-

ed into coins or other uses. A few works dating from the 16th century survive, mainly in silver, as evidence of skill in metalworking. These include a lovely little plateresque reliquary with sectioned columns and angels that the wealthy mine owner Alonso de Villaseca had made for him in 1578. There are also monstrances, chalices with bells, ciboriums, crosses and candlesticks, domestic utensils and jewelry. Dating from the 17th and 18th centuries there are also sacred vessels and other objects in engraved and embossed silver, sometimes gilded. Lamps and candelabras should not be forgotten. All these items are in churches and certain museums. In Morelia cathedral, a baptismal font and a large mon-

strance are all that remain of its wealth in silver. Gold church vessels and other religious objects, and also jewelry, survive in museums and private collections. Other metals were worked too, such as iron, copper, bronze and brass. The first of these was used for balconies and grilles especially for the chapels of some churches. There are also magnificent examples of beautifully worked lock escutcheons. Brass and bronze were used for candlesticks, inkwells, lamps or chandeliers, while saucepans, jugs, skillets and other cooking utensils were made of copper.

FURNITURE. The furniture brought by the Spanish was enriched or replaced by the influence of that used by the natives of New Spain. Because of the perishable nature of the materials used, little furniture remains from the 16th century; slightly more from the 17th century, and some excellent examples dating from the 18th century. Baroque furniture was influenced by the taste for cabriole legs and ball-and-claw feet, as well as for undulating sills. Fine examples of sacristy and domestic tables survive; chests for clothing, china and valuables were common. Wardrobes made their appearance later, and there are some fine examples of 18th-century carved works in Querétaro museum and in the cathedral of Tepic, Nayarit. Certain choirs in cathedrals and convent churches still retain their original stalls dating from the 16th to 19th centuries.

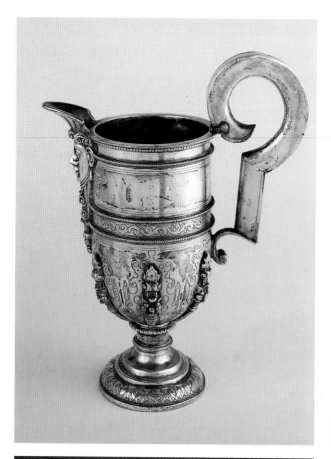

Above left. Engraved, embossed and gold-plated sliver pitcher. Seventeenth century, Private collection.

Above right. Christ Blessing or Divine Savior. A 16th-century feather mosaic, the finest known until now. National Viceroyal Museum, Tepotzotlán, State of Mexico.

Excellent work in pierced iron. Eighteenth century. National History Museum, Chapultepec Castle, Mexico City.

Chest. These were commonly used in the viceregal period for storing and transporting clothes and pottery. Eighteenth century. Chapultepec Castle, Mexico City.

Large bowl of Puebla glazed pottery. Thick white enamel decorated in two shades of blue. Seventeenth century. Bello Museum, Puebla, Puebla.

STATES OF MEXICO

PACIFIC OCEAN

MEXICO

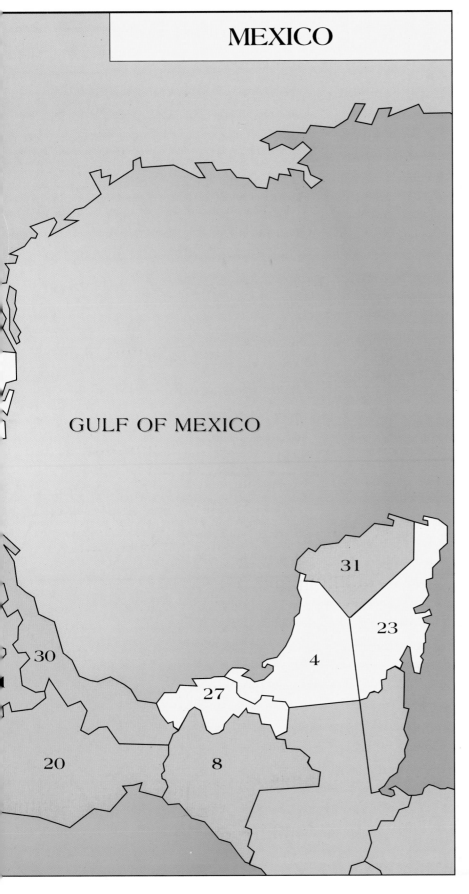

GULF OF MEXICO

1. Aguascalientes
2. Baja California
3. Baja California Sur
4. Campeche
5. Mexico City
6. Coahuila
7. Colima
8. Chiapas
9. Chihuahua
10. Durango
11. State of Mexico
12. Guanajuato
13. Guerrero
14. Hidalgo
15. Jalisco
16. Michoacán
17. Morelos
18. Nayarit
19. Nuevo León
20. Oaxaca
21. Puebla
22. Querétaro
23. Quintana Roo
24. San Luis Potosí
25. Sinaloa
26. Sonora
27. Tabasco
28. Tamaulipas
29. Tlaxcala
30. Veracruz
31. Yucatán
32. Zacatecas

COLONIAL MEXICO

Project and Concept: Casa Editrice Bonechi
Publication Manager: Monica Bonechi
Cover and Layout: Sonia Gottardo
Editing: Simonetta Giorgi

© Copyright by Casa Editrice Bonechi,
Via Cairoli 18b
Telf. +39 055576841 - Fax +39 0555000766
E-mail: bonechi@bonechi.it - Internet: www.bonechi.it
50131 Florence, Italy

ISBN 88-476-0062-6

COLONIAL MEXICO

Project and Concept: Monclem Ediciones
Publication Manager: Concepción Cadena
Cover and Layout: Angel Escobar
Editing: Angel Escobar
Translated by David B. Castledine

© Copyright by Monclem Ediciones, S.A. de C.V.
Leibnitz 31
Col. Anzures
11590 México, D.F.-México
Telf. 520 81 67 - Fax 202 88 14

ISBN 968-6434-72-0

Printed in Italy by
Centro Stampa Editoriale Bonechi

Distributor:
Monclem Ediciones S.A. de C.V.
Leibnitz 31
Col. Anzures
11590 México, D.F.-México
Telf 545 77 42
Fax 203 46 57

* * *

The Author.
Eugenio Noriega Robles, an expert in Mexican Colonial Art, was director of the National Viceroyal Museum of the National Institute of the National Institute of Anthropology, where he held several different positions, and professor of world history, the history of Mexico and the history of cultures. He is also the author of numerous books and articles on colonial art.

PHOTOGRAPHS:

G. Dagli Orti, pages: 4, 7, 8, 9 above and below, 10 above and below, 11 above and below, 12 above and below, 13, 14 above and below, 15 above and below, 16, 17, 18, 20 above, 22 below, 23 above and below, 24 above, 26, 27 below, 28, 29, 30 above and below, 31, 32 above and below, 33, 34 left, 35 above, 36 above and below 37, 38 above and below, 39 above and below 40 above and below, 41, 42, 43, 44 above and below, 45 above and below, 47 above and below, 48 above and below, 49, 50 above and below, 51 above and below, 52, 53 above and below, 54, 55, 56, 57 above and below, 58, 59 above and below, 60 above and below, 61, 64 below, 66 above and below, 67, 69 above, 70 above and below, 71, 73 above and below, 74, 75, 77 above and below, 78 below, 79, 80, 81 above and below, 83, 84 above and below, 85, 86 above and below, 87, 88 above and below, 92 above and below, 93 above and below and 94.

Walter Reuter, pages: 22 above, 24 below, 64 above, 89 above and below, 91, 96, 98 above, 103 above, 104, 107, 108 above right and 109 below.

B. Schalkwyk, pages: 5 and 6 above and below.

Michael Calderwood, pages: 46,62-63 and 68-69.

Jorge Vertiz, pages: 63 above, 103 below, 105 above right and 108 above left.

Alberto Ríos, pages: 27 above and 78 above.

Javier Hinojosa, pages: 101 above and 108 below.

Michel Zabe, pages: 109 above.

Guillermo Aldana, pages: 95 above right and 97 above.

Lourdes Grobet, pages: 35 below.

Archives Hachette Latinoamérica, pages: 19, 20 below, 21 above and below, 25 above and below, 34 right, 65, 72 above and below, 76 above and below, 82 above and below, 95 left above and below, 97 below, 98 below, 99, 100 above and below, 102 y 105 above left.

Archives Monclem, pages: 90 above and below et 106.

MUSEUMS:

Museo Nacional del Virreinato. Tepotzotlán.
Museo Nacional de Historia, Castillo
  de Chapultepec. Mexico City.
Pinacoteca Virreinal. Mexico City.
Museo Franz Mayer. Mexico City.
Museo Regional. Querétaro.
Museo Bello. Puebla.
Private collections.